Never Forget The Difference You've Made

44520858R00062

Made in the USA
San Bernardino, CA
20 July 2019